About the Author

Almost thirty years in the trenches of financial technology hasn't dimmed my excitement for what's next. I'm still a curious technologist exploring the potential of AI to transform the financial services landscape. This book, born from my AI exploration, showcases one powerful use case: how AI can reshape everyday operations documentation. Come with me on this journey – let's discover the future of finance, one revolutionized process at a time.

My passion lies in crafting groundbreaking, reliable, and secure solutions. Years of experience in architectural design and system orchestration have honed my ability to translate complex theories into practical systems. I navigate the ever-evolving tech landscape with ease, enabling organizations to extract actionable insights and thrive in the digital age.

But even seasoned veterans like me recognize the need for clear, accessible knowledge. In this book, I combine my practical experience, with an AI-powered approach to curate and distill complex information into a readily digestible form. Think of me as your guide, using AI as a tool to navigate the often-murky waters of financial technology documentation.

This book isn't just for me – it's for all the new faces thrust into the world of Fintech, yearning for a crash course in navigating its intricacies. By sharing my journey, I hope to demystify AI's potential in generating documentation and equip you with the knowledge to embrace these transformative technologies with confidence.

Disclaimer

The information contained in this book is for informational purposes only and is not intended to be a substitute for professional advice. While all attempts have been made to verify the information provided, the author and publisher make no warranties, express or implied, with respect to its accuracy, completeness, or timeliness.

The authors and publisher shall not be liable for any damages arising out of the use of the information contained in this book. This includes, but is not limited to, damages for errors, omissions, or technical inaccuracies.
Readers are encouraged to seek professional guidance relevant to their specific circumstances before making any decisions or taking any actions based on the information contained in this book.

FAIR USE DISCLAIMER:

This book discusses ServiceNow® products and functionalities for the purpose of education and commentary. References to ServiceNow® trademarks and copyrighted materials are made under the fair use doctrine with the sole intention of providing a comprehensive and informative exploration of ServiceNow® as a platform for IT service management (ITSM). The author and publisher do not claim any rights of ownership to the ServiceNow® trademarks or copyrighted materials.

Contents

INTRODUCTION

In today's dynamic business landscape, efficient and optimized operations are no longer a luxury, but a necessity. Organizations must strive for continuous service excellence to remain competitive. ServiceNow emerges as a powerful platform, designed to empower businesses to achieve this very goal. More than just software, ServiceNow offers a comprehensive suite of tools that can fundamentally transform your business processes and foster a culture of exceptional service delivery.

This book serves as your comprehensive guide to mastering ServiceNow. We'll embark on a detailed exploration of its core functionalities, equipping you to unlock its full potential and drive significant improvements across key areas like IT service management (ITSM), IT business management (ITBM), and IT operations management (ITOM).

Whether you're a seasoned IT professional or embarking on your ServiceNow journey for the first time, this book empowers you to:

- **Gain a Solid Foundation in ServiceNow:** We'll establish a strong understanding of the ServiceNow platform and its core functionalities. You'll gain insights into the foundational concepts of ITSM, ITBM, and ITOM, and how ServiceNow unifies these disciplines to create a holistic service management experience.

- **Navigate a Successful ServiceNow Implementation:** A well-planned ServiceNow implementation is crucial for maximizing its benefits. We'll guide you through a strategic approach that involves identifying your business needs, selecting the right ServiceNow products, and establishing a clear roadmap for implementation.
- **Optimize Core ServiceNow Functions:** Delve deep into core ServiceNow functionalities like incident, problem, change, and service request management. Through practical guidance, you'll learn how to optimize these functionalities to streamline workflows and empower your teams to deliver exceptional IT services.
- **Unlock the Value of ITBM:** ITBM within ServiceNow offers a powerful tool for gaining financial transparency and managing service costs effectively. We'll show you how to leverage ServiceNow to establish a robust service catalog that delivers standardized services across your organization.
- **Master IT Operations Management (ITOM):** We'll equip you to proactively monitor and manage your IT infrastructure using ServiceNow's event management, incident correlation, and configuration management database (CMDB) functionalities.

Beyond the core functionalities, this book equips you to:

- **Automate Workflows and Enhance Efficiency:** Leverage ServiceNow's automation capabilities and pre-built automations to streamline processes and significantly reduce manual effort.

- **Seamless Integration with Third-Party Applications:** We'll explore how to integrate ServiceNow with third-party applications to create a unified ecosystem that fosters seamless data flow across your organization.
- **Harness the Power of the ServiceNow Community:** Tap into the vast resources of the ServiceNow community to learn from industry experts and share your knowledge, fostering continuous learning and improvement.

Security and governance best practices will also be explored, ensuring the safe and compliant use of ServiceNow within your organization.

Chapter 1: Unveiling the Powerhouse of Service Management: A Deep Dive

The digital arena is a battlefield where efficiency reigns supreme. Businesses that can consistently deliver exceptional service and streamline operations emerge victorious. In this dynamic landscape, ServiceNow stands out as a powerful weapon in your arsenal, a comprehensive platform designed to empower organizations to achieve just that. This opening chapter serves as your portal to understanding ServiceNow's multifaceted functionalities and its transformative potential.

We'll embark on a detailed exploration, dissecting the core functionalities that make ServiceNow such a compelling solution. We'll delve into the foundational concepts of IT service management (ITSM), IT business management (ITBM), and IT operations management (ITOM), the three pillars upon which ServiceNow is built. You'll gain a clear understanding of how ServiceNow seamlessly integrates these disciplines, fostering a holistic service management experience within your organization. This integrated approach enables a culture of continuous improvement, ensuring your service delivery remains exceptional in the face of ever-evolving business needs.

But ServiceNow's value extends far beyond mere functionality. This chapter will shed light on the significant benefits of implementing ServiceNow within your organization. We'll uncover how the platform can revolutionize your workflows, transforming them into streamlined processes that maximize efficiency. You'll learn how ServiceNow optimizes resource allocation, ensuring your teams have the tools and resources they need to deliver exceptional service consistently. We'll explore how the platform empowers data-driven decision making, allowing you to identify areas for improvement and continuously refine your service delivery strategy.

By the conclusion of this chapter, you'll be equipped with a deep understanding of the power ServiceNow holds and the immense value it can bring to your business. You'll be prepared to embark on your ServiceNow journey with a clear vision of the transformative potential it offers, ready to unlock a new era of streamlined

The digital arena is a battlefield where efficiency reigns supreme. Businesses that can consistently deliver exceptional service and streamline operations emerge victorious. In this dynamic landscape, ServiceNow stands out as a powerful weapon in your arsenal, a comprehensive platform designed to empower organizations to achieve just that. This opening chapter serves as your portal to understanding ServiceNow's multifaceted functionalities and its transformative potential.

We'll embark on a detailed exploration, dissecting the core functionalities that make ServiceNow such a compelling solution. We'll delve into the foundational concepts of IT service management (ITSM), IT business management (ITBM), and IT operations management (ITOM), the three pillars upon which ServiceNow is built. You'll gain a clear understanding of how ServiceNow seamlessly integrates these disciplines, fostering a holistic service management experience within your organization. This integrated approach enables a culture of continuous improvement, ensuring your service delivery remains exceptional in the face of ever-evolving business needs.

But ServiceNow's value extends far beyond mere functionality. This chapter will shed light on the significant benefits of implementing ServiceNow within your organization. We'll uncover how the platform can revolutionize your workflows, transforming them into streamlined processes that maximize efficiency. You'll learn how ServiceNow optimizes resource allocation, ensuring your teams have the tools and resources they need to deliver exceptional service consistently. We'll explore how the platform empowers data-driven decision making, allowing you to identify areas for improvement and continuously refine your service delivery strategy.

By the conclusion of this chapter, you'll be equipped with a deep understanding of the power ServiceNow holds and the immense value it can bring to your business. You'll be prepared to embark on your ServiceNow journey with a clear vision of the transformative potential it offers, ready to unlock a new era of streamlined operations and exceptional service delivery within your organization.

1.1: Unveiling the ServiceNow Platform: A Deep Dive

ServiceNow stands as a cloud-based, comprehensive platform designed to empower organizations to streamline IT service management and broader business operations. This subchapter delves into the core functionalities of ServiceNow, providing a foundational understanding of its capabilities.

At its heart, ServiceNow is a Software-as-a-Service (SaaS) offering. This means the platform is hosted by the vendor, eliminating the need for extensive on-premise infrastructure setup and maintenance on your end. This cloud-based approach fosters scalability and accessibility, allowing you to access ServiceNow's functionalities from anywhere with an internet connection.

ServiceNow offers a wide range of built-in functionalities, catering to various aspects of service management. These functionalities can be broadly categorized into three core disciplines:

- **IT Service Management (ITSM):** This discipline focuses on the delivery and management of IT services within your organization. ServiceNow's ITSM functionalities encompass incident, problem, change, and service request management, providing a structured framework for resolving IT issues, identifying and preventing recurring problems, managing changes to the IT infrastructure effectively, and fulfilling user requests efficiently.

- **IT Business Management (ITBM):** ITBM extends beyond the realm of IT services, focusing on the alignment of IT with overall business goals. ServiceNow's ITBM functionalities include financial management, service catalog management, and service level management (SLM). These functionalities empower you to gain financial transparency regarding IT operations, establish a standardized catalog of IT services offered to the business, and define clear performance expectations for service delivery.
- **IT Operations Management (ITOM):** ITOM centers on proactively monitoring and managing your IT infrastructure. ServiceNow's ITOM functionalities encompass event management, incident correlation, and configuration management (CMDB). These functionalities enable you to proactively identify and address potential issues within your IT infrastructure, correlate events to identify root causes faster, and maintain an accurate inventory of all IT components.

By seamlessly integrating these three core disciplines, ServiceNow fosters a holistic service management experience. This integrated approach ensures that IT services are aligned with business needs, delivered efficiently, and continuously optimized for maximum value.

Throughout this book, we'll delve deeper into each of these core functionalities, equipping you with the knowledge and skills to leverage ServiceNow's full potential and transform your service delivery landscape.

1.2: Core Functionalities of ServiceNow (ITSM, ITBM, ITOM)

In subchapter 1.1, we explored the foundational aspects of the ServiceNow platform, highlighting its cloud-based nature and core service management disciplines: ITSM, ITBM, and ITOM. Now, let's delve deeper into the functionalities offered within each of these disciplines:

1. **IT Service Management (ITSM):**
    - **Incident Management:** ServiceNow's incident management functionality provides a structured framework for identifying, resolving, and reporting IT incidents (unexpected disruptions to IT services). It empowers your teams to log incidents efficiently, track their resolution progress, and ensure timely restoration of services.
    - **Problem Management:** This functionality focuses on identifying the root cause of recurring incidents and implementing preventative measures to avoid future occurrences. ServiceNow facilitates problem identification, analysis, and resolution, eliminating the need to "fight fires" repeatedly and ensuring long-term service stability.
    - **Change Management:** Managing changes to your IT infrastructure is

crucial to maintaining service stability. ServiceNow's change management functionality provides a structured approach for proposing, reviewing, approving, and implementing changes, minimizing the risk of disruptions and ensuring changes are implemented effectively.
- **Service Request Management:** This functionality streamlines the process of fulfilling user requests for IT services, such as access requests, software installations, or password resets. ServiceNow allows users to submit requests electronically, automates approval workflows, and facilitates efficient service delivery.

2. **IT Business Management (ITBM):**
   - **Financial Management:** Gaining financial transparency into IT operations is essential for informed decision-making. ServiceNow's financial management functionality helps you track IT costs associated with hardware, software, personnel, and other resources. This enables you to optimize resource allocation, identify areas for cost reduction, and demonstrate the business value of IT.
   - **Service Catalog Management:** A standardized service catalog is vital for ensuring consistent and efficient service delivery. ServiceNow allows you to create a catalog of IT services offered to the business, complete with detailed

descriptions, pricing information, and clear service level agreements (SLAs).

- **Service Level Management (SLM):** SLM defines the agreed-upon performance expectations for IT services. ServiceNow's SLM functionality facilitates the creation, monitoring, and reporting on SLAs, ensuring both IT and business stakeholders are aligned on service delivery expectations.

3. **IT Operations Management (ITOM):**
   - **Event Management:** Proactive monitoring of your IT infrastructure is essential for identifying and addressing potential issues before they disrupt services. ServiceNow's event management functionality allows you to collect and analyze events from various IT components, identify anomalies, and trigger alerts for timely intervention.
   - **Incident Correlation:** IT environments can generate a high volume of events. ServiceNow's incident correlation functionality helps you correlate seemingly unrelated events to identify the root cause of incidents faster, reducing resolution times and minimizing service downtime.
   - **Configuration Management Database (CMDB):** Maintaining an accurate inventory of all IT components within your infrastructure is crucial for effective management. ServiceNow's CMDB provides a centralized repository for configuration data, allowing you to track

hardware, software, network devices, and their relationships, ensuring a holistic view of your IT landscape.

By understanding these core functionalities, you'll gain a clear picture of how ServiceNow empowers organizations to manage IT services, align IT with business goals, and proactively manage their IT infrastructure. This integrated approach lays the foundation for achieving exceptional service delivery and driving continuous improvement within your organization.

1.3: Unveiling the Benefits of Implementing ServiceNow

In the previous subchapters, we explored the core functionalities of ServiceNow, delving into the three pillars of ITSM, ITBM, and ITOM. Now, let's shift our focus to the compelling benefits that implementing ServiceNow can bring to your organization.

1. Streamlined Workflows and Increased Efficiency:

ServiceNow replaces manual processes with automated workflows, significantly reducing the time and effort required to manage IT services. Incident resolution becomes faster, service requests are fulfilled efficiently, and changes are implemented with greater control. This streamlining translates to increased productivity for your IT teams, allowing them to focus on more strategic initiatives.

2. Improved Service Delivery and User Satisfaction:

By automating routine tasks and providing a centralized platform for managing service requests, ServiceNow empowers your IT teams to deliver services consistently and efficiently. Users benefit from a self-service portal for submitting requests and tracking their progress, leading to a more positive service experience and improved user satisfaction.

3. Enhanced Visibility and Control:

ServiceNow provides a comprehensive view of your IT infrastructure and service delivery processes. Real-time dashboards and reports empower informed decision-making, allowing you to identify areas for improvement and optimize resource allocation. Proactive monitoring capabilities within ITOM enable you to anticipate potential issues before they disrupt services, minimizing downtime and ensuring service continuity.

4. Increased Cost Savings and Resource Optimization:

ServiceNow's financial management tools provide valuable insights into IT costs. This transparency allows you to identify areas for cost reduction and optimize resource allocation, ensuring your IT budget is used effectively. Additionally, automation reduces the need for manual tasks, freeing up valuable IT staff resources for more strategic work.

5. Improved Collaboration and Communication:

ServiceNow fosters collaboration across teams by providing a centralized platform for communication and information sharing. This streamlines workflows, eliminates information silos, and ensures everyone involved has access to the latest information.

6. Scalability and Flexibility:

ServiceNow is a cloud-based platform, offering inherent scalability and flexibility. You can easily adapt the platform to your organization's evolving needs, adding new functionalities or expanding user access as required. This ensures ServiceNow remains a valuable tool as your business grows and your IT landscape matures.

7. Continuous Improvement and Innovation:

ServiceNow offers a robust reporting and analytics suite, enabling you to track key performance indicators (KPIs) and identify areas for improvement. This data-driven approach fosters a culture of continuous improvement, allowing you to refine your service delivery processes and ensure they remain aligned with your organization's strategic goals.

By implementing ServiceNow, you gain a powerful platform that streamlines workflows, optimizes resource allocation, and empowers exceptional service delivery. The benefits extend far beyond the IT department, fostering improved user satisfaction, cost savings, and a culture of continuous improvement within your organization.

Chapter 2: Charting Your Course: Planning a Successful ServiceNow Implementation

Having unveiled the power of ServiceNow in Chapter 1, we now set our sights on a successful implementation. Just like any voyage, embarking on a ServiceNow journey requires careful planning and a well-defined course. This chapter equips you with the essential tools to navigate the planning stages effectively.

We'll begin by guiding you through the process of identifying your business needs. A clear understanding of your pain points and desired outcomes is paramount for a successful ServiceNow implementation. We'll explore various strategies to assess your current state and define your target goals.

Next, we'll delve into selecting the right ServiceNow products. ServiceNow offers a vast array of functionalities, and choosing the ones that best align with your specific needs is crucial. We'll provide a framework for evaluating different ServiceNow modules and tailoring your selection to maximize the platform's value for your organization.

Finally, we'll explore strategies for building a winning implementation plan. This plan will serve as your roadmap to success, outlining key milestones, timelines, and resource allocation. We'll provide best practices for establishing a strong governance structure and ensuring clear communication throughout the implementation process.

By following the guidance outlined in this chapter, you'll lay a solid foundation for a successful ServiceNow implementation. A well-planned journey is half the battle won, and this chapter equips you with the tools and knowledge to chart a clear course towards achieving your service management goals with ServiceNow.

2.1: Identifying Your Business Needs: Charting the Course for Success

A successful ServiceNow implementation hinges on a deep understanding of your organization's specific needs and goals. Before embarking on this journey, it's crucial to take a step back and assess your current landscape. This subchapter equips you with the tools to identify your business needs and define clear objectives for your ServiceNow implementation.

1. Evaluating Your Current State:

The first step involves conducting a thorough self-assessment of your existing IT service management practices. Here are some key areas to consider:

- **Pain Points:** Identify the challenges you're currently facing with IT service delivery. Are you experiencing long resolution times for incidents? Is there a lack of transparency in your service request process? Pinpointing these pain points will highlight areas where ServiceNow can offer significant improvement.

- **Process Inefficiencies:** Are your IT service management processes manual and time-consuming? Do you have limited visibility into your IT infrastructure? Identifying these inefficiencies will help you understand how ServiceNow's automation and reporting capabilities can streamline workflows and improve visibility.
- **User Satisfaction:** How satisfied are your users with the current level of IT service delivery? Are they experiencing difficulties in submitting service requests or tracking their progress? Understanding user pain points will enable you to leverage ServiceNow's self-service portal and improved communication tools to enhance user experience.

2. Defining Your Target Goals:

Once you have a clear picture of your current state, it's time to define your desired future state. What are you hoping to achieve by implementing ServiceNow? Here are some potential goals to consider:

- **Improved Efficiency:** Do you aim to reduce incident resolution times or streamline service request fulfillment? Define measurable targets for efficiency improvements you hope to achieve with ServiceNow.
- **Enhanced User Satisfaction:** Is your goal to improve user experience by providing a self-service portal and transparent communication regarding service requests? Set clear objectives for user satisfaction that ServiceNow can help you achieve.

- **Cost Reduction:** Do you aim to optimize resource allocation or gain greater transparency into IT spending? Define goals for cost reduction that ServiceNow's financial management tools can support.
- **Proactive IT Management:** Is your objective to gain better visibility into your IT infrastructure and identify potential issues before they disrupt services? Set clear goals for proactive IT management that ServiceNow's ITOM functionalities can facilitate.

By conducting a thorough self-assessment and defining clear target goals, you'll gain a roadmap for your ServiceNow implementation. Understanding your current state and your desired future state ensures that your ServiceNow implementation addresses your specific needs and drives measurable improvements for your organization.

2.2: Choosing the Right ServiceNow Products: Aligning Functionalities with Needs

ServiceNow offers a comprehensive suite of functionalities, but not every organization needs them all. In this subchapter, we'll guide you through the process of selecting the right ServiceNow products to perfectly align with your identified business needs (defined in subchapter 2.1). Making informed choices ensures you maximize the value of your ServiceNow investment and avoid implementing functionalities that won't be optimally utilized.

1. Evaluating ServiceNow Products:

ServiceNow can be broadly categorized into the three core disciplines we explored in Chapter 1: ITSM, ITBM, and ITOM. Here's a breakdown of some key functionalities within each discipline:

- **IT Service Management (ITSM):**
  - Incident Management
  - Problem Management
  - Change Management
  - Service Request Management
- **IT Business Management (ITBM):**
  - Financial Management
  - Service Catalog Management
  - Service Level Management (SLM)
- **IT Operations Management (ITOM):**
  - Event Management
  - Incident Correlation
  - Configuration Management Database (CMDB)

2. Aligning Functionalities with Needs:

Refer back to the business needs you identified in subchapter 2.1. For each pain point or desired improvement, evaluate which ServiceNow functionalities can directly address them. Here's a framework to guide your selection process:

- **Identify the Need:** Clearly define the specific challenge you're aiming to address (e.g., slow incident resolution times).
- **Evaluate Relevant Functionalities:** Analyze which ServiceNow functionalities can directly contribute to resolving the need (e.g., Incident

Management for streamlined incident tracking and resolution).
- **Consider Business Impact:** Assess the potential impact of implementing the functionalities. Will it significantly improve efficiency, user satisfaction, or cost reduction?
- **Prioritize Needs:** Not all needs carry the same weight. Prioritize functionalities based on their potential impact and alignment with your overall business goals.

3. Leverage ServiceNow Resources:

ServiceNow offers a plethora of resources to help you navigate product selection. Here are some valuable tools:

- **ServiceNow Product Documentation:** Provides detailed information on the functionalities and capabilities of each product.
- **ServiceNow Product Demos:** Explore interactive demos to gain a firsthand look at how specific products work.
- **ServiceNow Success Stories:** Learn from real-world examples of how organizations have leveraged specific ServiceNow products to achieve their goals.

By following this structured approach, you'll make informed decisions about which ServiceNow products to implement. Remember, it's not about implementing everything; it's about choosing the functionalities that directly address your unique business needs and deliver the most significant value for your organization.

2.3: Building a Successful Implementation Strategy: Charting Your Course to ServiceNow Nirvana

With your business needs identified and ServiceNow products chosen, it's time to chart the course for a successful implementation. This subchapter equips you with the tools to build a winning implementation strategy, ensuring a smooth transition and maximizing the value you gain from ServiceNow.

1. Defining Key Milestones and Timelines:

A well-defined roadmap with clear milestones keeps your implementation on track. Here's what to consider:

- **Project Initiation:** Establish the project scope, define roles and responsibilities, and secure necessary resources.
- **Configuration and Customization:** Configure ServiceNow functionalities to align with your specific needs and business processes.
- **Data Migration (Optional):** If transitioning data from existing systems, plan and execute a comprehensive data migration strategy.
- **User Training and Adoption:** Develop a comprehensive training program to ensure users are comfortable and proficient in using ServiceNow.
- **Testing and Go-Live:** Thoroughly test the functionality of ServiceNow before launching it to your user base.
- **Post-Implementation Support:** Establish a plan for ongoing support and continuous improvement after go-live.

2. Establishing a Strong Governance Structure:

Effective governance ensures clear decision-making and accountability throughout the implementation process. Here are key elements of a strong governance structure:

- **Executive Sponsorship:** Secure the backing of an executive sponsor who champions the ServiceNow implementation and can provide strategic direction.
- **Project Steering Committee:** Form a committee with representatives from IT, business stakeholders, and project management to oversee the implementation and make key decisions.
- **Change Management Team:** Establish a dedicated team to manage the change process and ensure user adoption of ServiceNow.

3. Fostering Clear Communication and Collaboration:

Open communication throughout the implementation process is crucial. Here are some strategies to foster collaboration:

- **Regular Stakeholder Meetings:** Keep stakeholders informed with regular updates on project progress and address any concerns.
- **User Communication Plan:** Develop a communication plan to inform users about upcoming changes, training opportunities, and the benefits of ServiceNow implementation.
- **Collaboration Tools:** Leverage collaboration tools like wikis and communication channels to facilitate information sharing and team discussions.

By following these guidelines, you'll build a robust implementation strategy that sets your ServiceNow journey on the path to success. A clear roadmap, strong governance, and open communication will ensure a smooth transition and empower your organization to reap the full benefits of the ServiceNow platform.

Part 2: Optimizing Core ServiceNow Functions

Chapter 3: Mastering the Heart of Service Delivery: IT Service Management (ITSM) with ServiceNow

IT service management (ITSM) forms the cornerstone of exceptional service delivery. In this chapter, we delve into the ITSM functionalities within ServiceNow, empowering you to optimize core processes and deliver exceptional IT services to your users.

We'll begin by revisiting the foundational concepts of ITSM, exploring the key processes of incident, problem, change, and service request management. We'll then delve into how ServiceNow streamlines these processes, providing a structured framework for efficient service delivery.

Throughout this chapter, you'll gain practical guidance on:

- **Optimizing incident management:** Learn how to leverage ServiceNow to resolve incidents faster, minimize downtime, and improve user satisfaction.
- **Proactive problem management:** Explore how ServiceNow empowers you to identify the root cause of incidents and prevent them from recurring, ensuring long-term service stability.

- **Effective change management:** Discover how ServiceNow facilitates the implementation of changes to your IT infrastructure in a controlled and risk-minimized manner.
- **Streamlined service request management:** Uncover how ServiceNow empowers you to fulfill user requests for IT services efficiently and consistently.

By mastering these core ITSM functionalities within ServiceNow, you'll transform your IT service delivery landscape. This chapter equips you with the knowledge and skills to deliver exceptional service, minimize disruptions, and ensure your IT infrastructure remains a valuable asset to your organization.

3.1: Incident Management: Streamlining Issue Resolution with ServiceNow

Incidents – unexpected disruptions to IT services – are inevitable. However, their impact on your users and business operations can be significantly minimized through efficient incident management. This subchapter delves into how ServiceNow empowers you to streamline incident resolution, restore services quickly, and ensure user satisfaction.

Understanding Incident Management:

Incident management is a structured process for identifying, logging, resolving, and reporting IT incidents. The goal is to restore normal service operation as quickly as possible while minimizing downtime and its associated negative impacts.

ServiceNow to the Rescue:

ServiceNow's incident management functionality provides a centralized platform for managing the entire incident lifecycle. Here's how it streamlines the process:

- **Simplified Incident Logging:** Users can easily submit incident reports through a self-service portal, providing detailed descriptions and relevant attachments.
- **Automated Workflows:** ServiceNow automates routine tasks, such as routing incidents to the appropriate teams based on predefined rules. This reduces manual effort and ensures faster response times.
- **Enhanced Collaboration:** ServiceNow facilitates communication and collaboration between IT teams working on resolving incidents. Team members can share updates, escalate issues if needed, and ensure everyone involved is on the same page.
- **Improved Visibility and Tracking:** Real-time dashboards and reports provide insights into incident trends, resolution times, and technician performance. This allows for continuous improvement and proactive identification of potential issues.

Optimizing Your ServiceNow Incident Management:

- **Define clear escalation procedures:** Establish a structured approach for escalating incidents based on severity or requiring specialized expertise.

- **Leverage knowledge base articles:** Build a comprehensive knowledge base of solutions to common incidents, empowering users to self-resolve issues and reducing the burden on IT teams.
- **Implement automated recovery actions:** For frequently occurring incidents, configure automated workflows to trigger predefined actions, such as restarting services or rerouting traffic.

By leveraging ServiceNow's functionalities and implementing these best practices, you'll transform your incident management process. Faster resolution times, improved communication, and proactive identification of potential issues will contribute to a significant reduction in downtime and a more positive user experience.

3.2: Problem Management: Proactively Identifying and Resolving the Root Cause with ServiceNow

While incident management focuses on resolving immediate disruptions, problem management delves deeper. It's about identifying the root cause of incidents and implementing preventative measures to stop them from recurring. This subchapter explores how ServiceNow empowers you to shift from reactive firefighting to proactive problem management, ensuring long-term service stability.

Understanding Problem Management:

Problem management is a systematic approach for analyzing incidents, identifying their root causes, and implementing solutions to prevent them from happening again. This proactive approach minimizes the overall impact of incidents on your IT infrastructure and user experience.

ServiceNow: Your Proactive Partner:

ServiceNow's problem management functionality provides a robust framework for identifying and resolving the root cause of incidents. Here's how it empowers you to move beyond reactive solutions:

- **Incident Trend Analysis:** ServiceNow leverages analytics to identify patterns and trends within reported incidents. This allows you to pinpoint recurring issues and prioritize problem-solving efforts.
- **Root Cause Identification:** ServiceNow facilitates the investigation of incidents, enabling you to gather relevant data, analyze potential causes, and identify the true root cause of the problem.
- **Problem Resolution Workflows:** Define structured workflows for resolving identified problems. This may involve implementing configuration changes, deploying patches, or updating documentation to prevent future occurrences.
- **Knowledge Base Integration:** Document solutions to resolved problems within ServiceNow's knowledge base. This empowers IT teams to access solutions quickly when

similar incidents arise and fosters a culture of continuous learning.

Optimizing Your ServiceNow Problem Management:

- **Establish clear problem identification criteria:** Define specific conditions that trigger a problem investigation, ensuring you focus resources on issues with the potential for high impact.
- **Foster a culture of root cause analysis:** Encourage IT teams to delve deeper than just immediate symptoms when resolving incidents. Understanding the root cause empowers them to implement lasting solutions.
- **Prioritize problem resolution based on impact:** Focus your efforts on resolving problems with the highest potential to disrupt critical services or cause significant user inconvenience.

By leveraging ServiceNow's functionalities and implementing these best practices, you'll transform your problem management strategy. Moving from reactive incident resolution to proactive problem identification will minimize disruptions, improve service stability, and empower your IT teams to focus on strategic initiatives.

3.3: Change Management: Ensuring Smooth and Controlled Transitions with ServiceNow

Change is inevitable in any IT environment. However, implementing changes without proper planning and control can lead to disruptions and unintended consequences. This subchapter explores how ServiceNow empowers you to manage changes effectively, minimizing risks and ensuring a smooth transition to your desired state.

Understanding Change Management:

Change management is a structured process for planning, implementing, reviewing, and approving changes to your IT infrastructure, applications, or services. The goal is to minimize risks associated with change, ensure successful implementation, and minimize disruptions to ongoing operations.

ServiceNow: Your Trusted Guide Through Change:

ServiceNow's change management functionality provides a centralized platform for managing the entire change lifecycle. Here's how it streamlines the process and minimizes risks:

- **Automated Workflows:** Define workflows for submitting change requests, conducting approvals, and notifying stakeholders throughout the change process. This reduces manual effort and ensures accountability.
- **Risk Assessment Tools:** ServiceNow facilitates risk assessment for proposed changes, allowing you to identify potential issues and implement mitigation strategies before implementation.
- **Impact Analysis:** Evaluate the potential impact of a change on various aspects of your IT environment and business operations. This

allows for informed decision-making and helps prioritize changes based on their risk-reward profile.

- **Version Control and Audit Trails:** Maintain a clear audit trail for all changes implemented, allowing for easy tracking of modifications and facilitating rollback procedures if necessary.

Optimizing Your ServiceNow Change Management:

- **Define clear change approval processes:** Establish approval workflows based on the complexity and potential impact of the change.
- **Standardize change templates:** Create pre-defined templates for common change types, streamlining the submission process and ensuring all necessary information is captured.
- **Foster communication and collaboration:** Ensure clear communication with stakeholders throughout the change process, keeping everyone informed and managing expectations.

By leveraging ServiceNow's functionalities and implementing these best practices, you'll ensure a smooth and controlled transition when implementing changes to your IT environment. Minimized risks, improved communication, and a focus on impact analysis will empower you to navigate change effectively and achieve your desired outcomes.

3.4: Service Request Management: Streamlining User Requests and Delivering Exceptional Service with ServiceNow

Empowering your users to request IT services efficiently is crucial for a positive service experience. This subchapter dives into ServiceNow's service request management functionality, equipping you to streamline user requests, optimize fulfillment processes, and deliver exceptional service.

Understanding Service Request Management:

Service request management is a structured process for handling user requests for IT services. This can encompass a wide range of requests, from access to software applications and hardware to resetting passwords and requesting new accounts.

ServiceNow: Simplifying Service Delivery:

ServiceNow's service request management functionality provides a self-service portal for users to submit requests electronically. Here's how it streamlines the process and improves user satisfaction:

- **Self-Service Portal:** Users can easily submit requests through a user-friendly interface, eliminating the need for emails or phone calls to the IT service desk.
- **Catalog of Services:** Maintain a standardized catalog of IT services offered, with clear descriptions, eligibility requirements, and

estimated completion times. This empowers users to find the service they need and understand the request process.

- **Automated Workflows:** Automate routine tasks associated with service requests, such as assigning requests to the appropriate teams and notifying users of updates.
- **Approval Workflows:** Implement approval workflows for specific service requests, ensuring proper authorization before service delivery.
- **Self-Service Knowledge Base:** Empower users to find answers to common questions and troubleshoot basic issues on their own through a self-service knowledge base integrated with the service request portal.

Optimizing Your ServiceNow Service Request Management:

- **Standardize service offerings:** Develop a clear and concise catalog of services offered, ensuring consistency and user understanding.
- **Categorize and prioritize requests:** Implement a system for categorizing and prioritizing service requests based on urgency and complexity.
- **Define service level agreements (SLAs):** Establish clear SLAs for different service requests, outlining timelines and expectations for service delivery.
- **Track and measure performance:** Utilize ServiceNow's reporting tools to track key performance indicators (KPIs) associated with service request management, allowing you to

identify areas for improvement and optimize your processes.

By leveraging ServiceNow's functionalities and implementing these best practices, you'll transform your service request management landscape. A user-friendly self-service portal, clear communication of service offerings, and efficient fulfillment processes will empower your users to get the IT support they need quickly and easily, leading to a more positive service experience.

Chapter 4: Bridging the Gap: IT Business Management (ITBM) with ServiceNow

In today's dynamic business landscape, IT plays a pivotal role in driving success. ITBM, or IT Business Management, emerges as the strategic bridge connecting IT services with overall business goals. This chapter delves into how ServiceNow empowers you to leverage ITBM practices, ensuring IT investments align with business objectives and deliver tangible value to your organization.

We'll begin by exploring the core concepts of ITBM, encompassing financial management, service catalog management, and service level management (SLM). We'll then delve into how ServiceNow facilitates the implementation of these practices, fostering a collaborative environment where IT and the business work together seamlessly.

Throughout this chapter, you'll gain practical guidance on:

- **Financial Transparency:** Uncover how ServiceNow empowers you to gain insights into IT costs and optimize resource allocation, ensuring your IT budget is used effectively.
- **Standardized Service Catalog:** Learn how to leverage ServiceNow to create a comprehensive service catalog, clearly defining the IT services offered to the business and their associated costs.

- **Effective Service Level Management:**
  Explore how ServiceNow facilitates the definition, monitoring, and reporting on SLAs, ensuring both IT and business stakeholders are aligned on service delivery expectations.

By mastering these core ITBM functionalities within ServiceNow, you'll transform your organization's approach to IT. ServiceNow empowers you to demonstrate the value of IT investments, foster collaboration between IT and the business, and ultimately drive strategic decision-making for long-term success.

4.1: Financial Management: Unveiling Costs and Optimizing Resources with ServiceNow

Understanding the true cost of IT services is crucial for informed decision-making and maximizing the value of your IT investments. This subchapter explores ServiceNow's financial management functionalities, empowering you to gain financial transparency, control IT costs, and optimize resource allocation.

Why Financial Management Matters in ITBM:

Traditionally, IT costs have been viewed as an expense to be minimized. However, ITBM takes a more strategic approach. By understanding the financial implications of IT services, you can demonstrate their value proposition, identify areas for cost savings, and ensure resources are allocated effectively to support business objectives.

ServiceNow: Your Financial Transparency Partner:

ServiceNow's financial management functionality provides a comprehensive suite of tools for tracking and analyzing IT costs. Here's how it empowers you to gain financial clarity:

- **Cost Tracking and Reporting:** Track IT costs associated with hardware, software, personnel, and other resources. ServiceNow allows you to categorize these costs by department, service offering, or project, facilitating granular cost analysis.
- **Showback and Chargeback:** Implement showback and chargeback mechanisms to allocate IT costs to specific business units or departments. This fosters accountability and encourages responsible use of IT services.
- **Budget Management:** Set budgets for IT spending and track expenses against those budgets in real-time. Identify potential cost overruns and make informed decisions to stay within budget constraints.
- **Return on Investment (ROI) Analysis:** Evaluate the financial benefits of IT investments by analyzing cost savings, improved efficiencies, and increased revenue generation associated with specific IT projects or services.

Optimizing Your ServiceNow Financial Management:

- **Develop a comprehensive cost tracking strategy:** Define a clear approach for capturing and categorizing all IT-related costs within ServiceNow.

- **Leverage automation:** Automate routine tasks associated with cost tracking and reporting, such as data collection and expense allocation.
- **Communicate cost insights effectively:** Share cost transparency reports with business stakeholders to foster collaboration and demonstrate the value proposition of IT investments.

By leveraging ServiceNow's financial management functionalities and implementing these best practices, you'll gain a clear picture of your IT spend. Financial transparency empowers you to identify cost-saving opportunities, optimize resource allocation, and make data-driven decisions that support your organization's strategic goals.

4.2: Service Catalog Management: Delivering Standardized Services with ServiceNow

A standardized service catalog forms the cornerstone of effective IT service delivery. This subchapter dives into ServiceNow's service catalog management functionalities, equipping you to create a clear and consistent catalog of IT services offered to the business. A well-defined catalog streamlines service requests, reduces confusion, and ensures both IT and business stakeholders are aligned on service offerings.

The Power of a Standardized Service Catalog:

A standardized service catalog serves multiple purposes:

- **Clarity for Users:** Users can easily find the IT services they need with clear descriptions, eligibility requirements, and estimated completion times. This reduces ambiguity and empowers users to submit accurate service requests.
- **Efficiency for IT Teams:** A standardized catalog ensures IT teams understand the scope of each service request, allowing them to fulfill requests efficiently and consistently.
- **Alignment Between IT and Business:** The service catalog fosters a common understanding of IT services offered and their associated costs. This transparency promotes collaboration and ensures IT investments are aligned with business needs.

ServiceNow: Your Service Catalog Champion:

ServiceNow provides a robust platform for building and managing your service catalog. Here's how it empowers you to deliver standardized services:

- **User-Friendly Catalog Interface:** Design a user-friendly catalog interface that allows users to browse services by category, keyword search, or department.
- **Standardized Service Descriptions:** Develop clear and concise descriptions for each service offered, outlining what it entails, who it's intended for, and any associated costs or limitations.

- **Automated Workflows:** Automate workflows associated with specific services within the catalog. This can include automatic service provisioning, user notifications, and task assignments to relevant IT teams.
- **Version Control and Audit Trails:** Maintain version control for your service catalog, ensuring all changes are documented and tracked. Audit trails allow you to understand historical changes and identify potential issues.

Optimizing Your ServiceNow Service Catalog Management:

- **Involve stakeholders in catalog development:** Collaborate with business units and IT teams to ensure the service catalog reflects the needs of both sides.
- **Maintain an evergreen catalog:** Regularly review and update your service catalog to reflect changes in IT offerings, pricing models, or business requirements.
- **Promote user awareness:** Educate users about the service catalog and how to access it. This empowers them to find the services they need and reduces reliance on IT for basic service requests.

By leveraging ServiceNow's functionalities and implementing these best practices, you'll create a standardized service catalog that serves as a central point of reference for both IT and the business. A clear and consistent catalog empowers users, streamlines service delivery, and fosters collaboration, ultimately leading to a more efficient and effective IT service management landscape.

4.3: Service Level Management (SLM): Defining, Monitoring, and Meeting Service Expectations with ServiceNow

Service Level Management (SLM) forms a critical aspect of ITBM. It ensures that IT services are delivered at a consistent and measurable level that meets the agreed-upon needs of the business. This subchapter explores how ServiceNow empowers you to implement effective SLM practices, define clear service expectations, and ensure consistent service delivery.

Understanding Service Level Management:

SLM establishes a framework for defining, agreeing upon, measuring, and reporting on the performance of IT services. This involves establishing Service Level Agreements (SLAs) that outline the specific service expectations for availability, performance, and responsiveness.

ServiceNow: Your SLM Champion:

ServiceNow provides a comprehensive suite of tools to facilitate effective SLM. Here's how it empowers you to manage service expectations:

- **SLA Definition and Management:** Define SLAs within ServiceNow, outlining service metrics, target levels, and consequences for not meeting those targets.
- **Automated Monitoring and Reporting:** Leverage ServiceNow's automation capabilities

to monitor IT service performance against agreed-upon SLAs. Generate real-time reports that provide insights into service availability, response times, and adherence to SLAs.

- **Exception Management:** Establish workflows for identifying and handling SLA breaches. ServiceNow can trigger alerts and notifications when service levels fall below expectations, allowing IT teams to take corrective action promptly.
- **Continuous Improvement:** Utilize ServiceNow's reporting tools to identify trends and analyze historical SLA data. This empowers you to identify areas for improvement and continuously refine your SLAs to better meet the evolving needs of the business.

Optimizing Your ServiceNow SLM:

- **Engage stakeholders in SLA development:** Collaborate with business units and IT teams to define SLAs that reflect realistic expectations and align with business priorities.
- **Communicate SLAs effectively:** Ensure all stakeholders are aware of established SLAs, understand their roles and responsibilities, and have access to SLA reports.
- **Regularly review and update SLAs:** Business needs and IT capabilities evolve over time. Review SLAs periodically to ensure they remain relevant and reflect current requirements.

By leveraging ServiceNow's functionalities and implementing these best practices, you'll transform your SLM practices. Clearly defined SLAs, automated monitoring, and a focus on continuous improvement will ensure IT services meet business expectations consistently. This fosters trust and collaboration between IT and the business, ultimately driving organizational success.

Chapter 5: Gaining End-to-End Visibility: IT Operations Management (ITOM) with ServiceNow

In today's complex IT landscape, maintaining visibility and control over your infrastructure is paramount. IT Operations Management (ITOM) empowers you to achieve this by providing a holistic view of your IT environment, from the physical hardware to the applications and services that run on it. This chapter delves into how ServiceNow's ITOM functionalities equip you to gain end-to-end visibility, optimize resource utilization, and proactively identify potential issues before they disrupt critical services.

We'll begin by exploring the core concepts of ITOM, encompassing configuration management, event management, and incident correlation. We'll then delve into how ServiceNow facilitates the implementation of these practices, empowering you to gain a comprehensive understanding of your IT environment and proactively manage its performance.

Throughout this chapter, you'll gain practical guidance on:

- **Maintaining an Accurate CMDB:** Discover how ServiceNow empowers you to build and maintain a Configuration Management Database (CMDB) that provides a single source of truth for all your IT assets and their interdependencies.

- **Real-Time Event Management:** Explore how ServiceNow facilitates the collection, correlation, and analysis of IT events, allowing you to identify potential issues and minimize downtime.
- **Proactive Incident Correlation:** Learn how ServiceNow leverages automation and machine learning to correlate event data and identify root causes of incidents before they escalate.

By mastering these core ITOM functionalities within ServiceNow, you'll transform your approach to IT operations. Enhanced visibility, proactive issue identification, and streamlined incident resolution will empower your IT teams to operate more efficiently, minimize disruptions, and ensure the smooth delivery of critical IT services to your organization.

5.1: Event Management: Proactively Identifying Issues with ServiceNow

IT environments are constantly generating a deluge of events – log messages, system alerts, application notifications. Sifting through this data to identify potential issues can be overwhelming. This subchapter explores ServiceNow's event management functionalities, empowering you to proactively monitor your IT infrastructure, identify potential problems early on, and minimize disruptions to your services.

Understanding Event Management:

Event management involves collecting, analyzing, and responding to events generated by IT devices, applications, and services. The goal is to identify potential problems early in their lifecycle, before they escalate into critical incidents that disrupt user productivity or business operations.

ServiceNow: Your Proactive Watchdog:

ServiceNow's event management functionality provides a centralized platform for collecting and analyzing event data from across your IT infrastructure. Here's how it empowers you to move from reactive firefighting to proactive problem identification:

- **Event Collection from Diverse Sources:** Leverage ServiceNow to collect event data from various sources, including network devices, servers, applications, and security systems.
- **Event Correlation and Normalization:** ServiceNow normalizes event data from disparate sources, allowing you to identify patterns and relationships between seemingly unrelated events.
- **Real-Time Alerting and Escalation:** Define automated alerting rules to trigger notifications for critical or potentially disruptive events. These alerts can be directed to the appropriate IT teams based on the severity and nature of the event.
- **Event Trend Analysis:** Utilize ServiceNow's reporting tools to analyze historical event data and identify trends. This empowers you to

predict potential issues and take preventative measures before they escalate.

Optimizing Your ServiceNow Event Management:

- **Prioritize event alerts:** Configure event rules to prioritize alerts based on severity, potential impact, and the urgency required for response.
- **Implement automated remediation actions:** For frequently occurring, low-risk events, define automated actions within ServiceNow to trigger self-healing processes or basic troubleshooting steps.
- **Foster collaboration between IT teams:** Ensure clear communication and collaboration protocols are established when responding to event alerts. This allows IT teams to work together effectively to resolve issues quickly.

By leveraging ServiceNow's functionalities and implementing these best practices, you'll transform your event management strategy. Proactive monitoring, intelligent event correlation, and automated alerting empower you to identify potential issues early and minimize their impact on your IT operations. This proactive approach ensures your IT environment remains stable and delivers consistent service to your users.

5.2: Incident Correlation: Unveiling the Root Cause Faster with ServiceNow

In the fast-paced world of IT operations, resolving incidents quickly and efficiently is crucial. However, pinpointing the root cause of an incident can be like finding a needle in a haystack, especially when dealing with complex IT environments. This subchapter explores ServiceNow's incident correlation functionalities, empowering you to automate the process of analyzing event data, identifying root causes faster, and resolving incidents with greater efficiency.

Understanding Incident Correlation:

Incident correlation involves analyzing data from various sources, such as event logs, network traffic, and system performance metrics, to identify the root cause of an incident. Traditionally, this process is manual and time-consuming, often delaying incident resolution and prolonging service disruptions.

ServiceNow: Your Automated Root Cause Detective:

ServiceNow's incident correlation functionality leverages automation and machine learning to streamline the process of identifying the root cause of incidents. Here's how it empowers you to expedite incident resolution:

- **Automated Event Aggregation and Analysis:** ServiceNow automatically collects event data associated with an incident from various sources and aggregates it into a centralized view.

- **Machine Learning-Powered Root Cause Identification:** ServiceNow utilizes machine learning algorithms to analyze event data and identify patterns or correlations that may point to the root cause of the incident.
- **Visualizations and Impact Analysis:** ServiceNow presents the correlated event data in an easy-to-understand visual format, allowing IT teams to quickly grasp the sequence of events and identify the potential root cause.
- **Integration with Incident Management:** Seamless integration with ServiceNow's incident management functionality allows you to link correlated events to the relevant incident record, streamlining the overall resolution process.

Optimizing Your ServiceNow Incident Correlation:

- **Define clear correlation rules:** Establish rules within ServiceNow to guide the analysis of event data and identify potential relationships between seemingly unrelated events.
- **Train the machine learning engine:** Over time, provide ServiceNow with historical incident data to enhance the

machine learning algorithms' ability to identify root causes accurately.

- **Focus on continuous improvement:** Regularly review incident correlation data and identify areas for improvement. Refine correlation rules and machine learning models to ensure they remain effective in pinpointing root causes.

By leveraging ServiceNow's functionalities and implementing these best practices, you'll transform your incident resolution process. Automated incident correlation empowers you to identify root causes faster, troubleshoot issues more effectively, and minimize the downtime associated with incidents. This translates to a more efficient IT operation and a more positive user experience.

5.3: Configuration Management Database (CMDB): Building a Single Source of Truth

Within any complex IT environment, maintaining an accurate and up-to-date inventory of all IT assets and their configurations is crucial. This subchapter explores ServiceNow's Configuration Management Database (CMDB) functionalities, empowering you to build a single source of truth for your IT infrastructure. A comprehensive CMDB forms the foundation for effective IT operations management, ensuring all stakeholders have a clear understanding of the IT landscape and its interdependencies.

Understanding Configuration Management:

Configuration management involves maintaining a detailed record of all IT assets within your organization, including hardware, software, applications, network devices, and virtual machines. This record encompasses not only the type and model of each asset but also its configuration settings, relationships with other assets, and lifecycle information.

ServiceNow: Your CMDB Champion:

ServiceNow provides a robust platform for building and maintaining your CMDB. Here's how it empowers you to create a single source of truth for your IT infrastructure:

- **Automated Asset Discovery and Reconciliation:** Leverage ServiceNow's automation capabilities to discover new IT assets within your network and automatically populate the CMDB. Regular reconciliation processes ensure the CMDB remains accurate and reflects any changes to your IT environment.
- **Standardized Configuration Items (CIs):** Define standardized CI classes within ServiceNow to represent different types of IT assets. This ensures consistency and facilitates reporting across the entire CMDB.
- **Relationship Modeling:** Map the relationships between different CIs within the CMDB. This allows you to visualize dependencies and understand how changes to one asset might impact others.

- **Version Control and Audit Trails:** Maintain version control for your CMDB entries, allowing you to track configuration changes over time. Audit trails provide a historical record of changes and facilitate troubleshooting efforts.

Optimizing Your ServiceNow CMDB:

- **Develop a comprehensive data collection strategy:** Define clear processes for gathering and maintaining accurate asset data within the CMDB.
- **Promote CMDB ownership across IT teams:** Encourage all IT teams to contribute to the CMDB by providing accurate and up-to-date information about the assets they manage.
- **Utilize CMDB data for strategic decision-making:** Leverage the rich data within the CMDB to inform IT purchasing decisions, optimize asset utilization, and support IT risk management initiatives.

By leveraging ServiceNow's functionalities and implementing these best practices, you'll build a reliable and accurate CMDB that serves as the foundation for effective IT operations management. A comprehensive CMDB empowers you to gain a holistic view of your IT environment, make data-driven decisions, and ensure all stakeholders have a clear understanding of your IT landscape.

Part 3: Enhancing Your ServiceNow Experience

Chapter 6: Automation Magic: Streamlining Workflows and Boosting Efficiency with ServiceNow

In today's dynamic IT landscape, manual processes can become bottlenecks, hindering productivity and hindering your ability to respond effectively to user needs. This chapter delves into the power of automation within ServiceNow. We'll explore how to leverage ServiceNow's workflow automation functionalities to streamline repetitive tasks, expedite service delivery, and empower your IT teams to focus on strategic initiatives.

Throughout this chapter, you'll discover:

- **The Power of Workflows:** Gain a comprehensive understanding of workflows and their role in automating routine tasks within ServiceNow.
- **Building Effective Workflows:** Learn best practices for designing and implementing efficient workflows that optimize your IT service management processes.
- **Advanced Automation Techniques:** Explore more sophisticated automation capabilities

within ServiceNow, such as scripting and custom integrations.

By harnessing the magic of automation, you'll transform your ServiceNow experience. Streamlined workflows, improved efficiency, and empowered IT teams will position your organization to achieve its IT service management goals and deliver exceptional service to your users.

6.1: Building Workflows with Flow Designer: Orchestrating Automation Magic

Imagine a world where routine IT service management tasks handle themselves, freeing your IT professionals to focus on more strategic initiatives. This is the power of workflow automation within ServiceNow, and Flow Designer is your key to making it a reality. This subchapter dives into the fundamentals of building effective workflows with Flow Designer, empowering you to streamline processes, minimize manual effort, and optimize your ServiceNow experience.

Understanding Workflows:

A workflow is a visual representation of a business process that outlines the sequence of steps required to complete a task. Within ServiceNow, workflows automate these steps, eliminating the need for manual intervention. Flow Designer provides a user-friendly drag-and-drop interface for building workflows, allowing you to orchestrate a series of activities triggered by specific events within ServiceNow.

Building Effective Workflows with Flow Designer:

- **Identify Repetitive Tasks:** The first step is to pinpoint repetitive tasks within your IT service management processes that are ideal candidates for automation. Consider tasks that are prone to human error or those that consume a significant amount of IT staff time.
- **Design Your Workflow:** Flow Designer provides a visual canvas where you can map out the sequence of steps involved in your workflow. You can drag and drop various activities, such as sending notifications, updating records, or invoking scripts, to define the desired automation sequence.
- **Define Conditions and Triggers:** Specify the conditions that will trigger the execution of your workflow. This could be a user submitting a specific service request, an incident being created, or a change record reaching a particular stage in its approval process.
- **Configure Activities:** For each activity within your workflow, define the specific actions to be performed. This may involve assigning tasks to specific users or groups, updating field values within ServiceNow records, or integrating with external systems.
- **Test and Refine:** Once your workflow is built, thoroughly test it within a non-production environment to ensure it functions as intended. Refine your workflow based on testing results and iterate until you achieve the desired level of automation.

Optimizing Your Workflow Design:

- **Keep it simple:** Start with automating well-defined, routine tasks. As you gain experience, gradually progress towards more complex workflows.
- **Leverage pre-built activities:** ServiceNow offers a library of pre-built workflow activities that cater to common tasks. Utilize these pre-built activities to streamline your workflow development process.
- **Document your workflows:** Clearly document the purpose, functionality, and trigger conditions of your workflows. This facilitates ongoing maintenance and ensures knowledge transfer within your IT teams.

By following these guidelines and leveraging the capabilities of Flow Designer, you'll be well on your way to building effective workflows that streamline your ServiceNow processes and empower your IT teams to achieve greater efficiency.

6.2: Leverage Pre-built Automations: Accelerating Efficiency with ServiceNow

Building workflows from scratch can be a time-consuming endeavor. Thankfully, ServiceNow offers a wealth of pre-built automations that address common IT service management tasks. This subchapter explores the advantages of leveraging pre-built automations and equips you to identify, implement, and customize these pre-configured workflows within your ServiceNow instance.

The Power of Pre-built Automations:

Pre-built automations are pre-designed workflows readily available within ServiceNow. They offer several advantages that can significantly enhance your ServiceNow experience:

- **Reduced Development Time:** Leveraging pre-built automations eliminates the need to build workflows from scratch, saving you valuable time and resources. This allows you to implement automation solutions quickly and efficiently.
- **Improved Efficiency:** Pre-built automations are designed to streamline common tasks, ensuring consistent and efficient execution of these processes within your IT service management framework.
- **Reduced Risk of Errors:** ServiceNow rigorously tests its pre-built automations, minimizing the risk of errors compared to custom-built workflows. This ensures reliable and predictable automation behavior.
- **Best Practice Implementation:** Pre-built automations often incorporate industry best practices for IT service management, ensuring your workflows are aligned with established standards.

Finding and Implementing Pre-built Automations:

- **Identify Your Needs:** The first step is to identify repetitive tasks or processes within your IT service management function that are suitable for automation. ServiceNow categorizes pre-built automations by functionality, making it easier to find relevant solutions.

- **Explore the ServiceNow Catalog:** Browse the ServiceNow platform's pre-built automation library. You can search by keyword or filter by category to find automations that align with your specific needs.
- **Evaluate and Implement:** Carefully evaluate each pre-built automation to ensure it addresses your requirements. Once you've identified a suitable automation, the implementation process is usually straightforward, often involving minimal configuration.

Customizing Pre-built Automations:

While pre-built automations offer a strong foundation, you can often customize them to perfectly fit your specific needs. Here's how you can tailor pre-built automations within ServiceNow:

- **Configure Parameters:** Many pre-built automations allow you to configure parameters to define specific details like notification recipients, approval requirements, or due dates.
- **Add Additional Activities:** In some cases, you may want to extend the functionality of a pre-built automation by adding additional activities to the workflow. ServiceNow's Flow Designer allows you to integrate custom activities seamlessly.

Optimizing Your Use of Pre-built Automations:

- **Standardize on pre-built automations:** Whenever possible, leverage pre-built automations to streamline common tasks and processes. This promotes consistency and reduces reliance on custom-built workflows that require ongoing maintenance.

- **Stay updated with new offerings:** ServiceNow regularly releases new pre-built automations. Stay informed about the latest additions to the library to identify opportunities to further streamline your IT service management processes.

By embracing pre-built automations and following these best practices, you'll significantly accelerate your automation journey within ServiceNow. Pre-built workflows empower you to achieve faster time-to-value, reduce development efforts, and ensure efficient execution of common IT service management tasks. This translates to a more streamlined and efficient IT service management experience for both your IT staff and your end-users.

6.3: Best Practices for Effective Automation: Building a Sustainable Automation Foundation with ServiceNow

Automation offers immense potential to transform your ServiceNow experience. However, implementing effective automation requires careful planning and a strategic approach. This subchapter explores best practices for building a sustainable automation foundation within ServiceNow, ensuring your automations deliver on their promise of efficiency and improved service delivery.

Laying the Groundwork for Effective Automation:

- **Identify the Right Processes to Automate:** Not all processes are ideal candidates for automation. Focus on tasks that are repetitive, rule-based, and prone to human error. Avoid automating complex, judgment-driven tasks that require human intervention.
- **Start Small and Scale Gradually:** Begin by automating a few well-defined tasks. As you gain experience and confidence, gradually expand your automation efforts to encompass more complex processes. This phased approach minimizes disruption and allows you to identify and address any challenges before scaling automation efforts.
- **Involve Stakeholders in the Process:** Ensure relevant stakeholders, including IT staff and end-users, are involved in the automation process. Their input can help identify suitable tasks for automation and ensure the workflows meet the needs of all users.
- **Clearly Define Success Metrics:** Before implementing an automation, establish clear metrics to measure its success. This may include factors such as time saved, improved accuracy, or increased efficiency. Tracking these metrics allows you to evaluate the effectiveness of your automations and identify areas for improvement.

Building and Maintaining Effective Automations:

- **Document Your Workflows:** Clearly document your workflows, outlining their purpose, functionality, and trigger conditions.

This facilitates ongoing maintenance and knowledge transfer within your IT teams.

- **Test Thoroughly:** Rigorously test your workflows in a non-production environment before deploying them in your live ServiceNow instance. This helps identify and rectify any errors before they can impact your users or critical processes.
- **Monitor and Refine:** Automation is an ongoing process. Continuously monitor the performance of your workflows and make adjustments as needed. Look for opportunities to further optimize your workflows and identify additional processes that can be automated.
- **Foster a Culture of Continuous Improvement:** Promote a culture of continuous improvement within your IT organization. Encourage feedback from stakeholders on existing automations and solicit suggestions for new automation opportunities.

Optimizing Your Automation Journey:

- **Invest in training:** Provide adequate training to IT staff on ServiceNow's automation functionalities, including Flow Designer. This empowers them to identify automation opportunities, build effective workflows, and troubleshoot any automation-related issues.
- **Standardize on automation best practices:** Establish clear guidelines and best practices for automation within your organization. This ensures consistency, quality, and maintainability of your automated workflows.

- **Measure the ROI of automation:** Track the return on investment (ROI) of your automation initiatives. By quantifying the benefits of automation, such as cost savings or improved efficiency, you can gain buy-in from stakeholders and secure funding for future automation projects.

By following these best practices and establishing a solid foundation for automation, you'll ensure your ServiceNow automations deliver sustainable value. Effective automation streamlines workflows, minimizes manual effort, and empowers your IT teams to focus on higher-level IT service management initiatives, ultimately driving improved service delivery and user satisfaction.

Chapter 7: Unleashing the Power of Integrations: Expanding Your ServiceNow Ecosystem

In today's interconnected IT landscape, no single platform exists in isolation. This chapter delves into the power of integrations within ServiceNow. We'll explore how to leverage ServiceNow's integration capabilities to connect your instance with other critical business systems, fostering seamless data exchange and streamlined workflows. By integrating ServiceNow with your existing IT ecosystem, you can:

- **Eliminate Data Silos:** Break down information barriers between ServiceNow and other applications, ensuring a unified view of your IT environment and business processes.
- **Automate Cross-Platform Workflows:** Orchestrate automated workflows that span multiple systems, eliminating the need for manual data entry and error-prone manual processes.
- **Enhance User Experience:** Provide a more seamless user experience by connecting ServiceNow with applications your users interact with daily.
- **Improve Decision Making:** Gain a holistic view of your data across various systems, empowering you to make data-driven decisions that optimize your IT service management practices.

Throughout this chapter, we'll explore the different types of integrations available within ServiceNow, dive into popular integration methods, and provide best practices for implementing successful and secure integrations. By harnessing the power of integrations, you'll transform ServiceNow from a stand-alone platform into a central hub that seamlessly connects your entire IT ecosystem, ultimately fostering greater efficiency and improving the overall value proposition of your ServiceNow investment.

7.1: Connecting ServiceNow with Third-Party Applications: Expanding Your IT Ecosystem

ServiceNow thrives in an interconnected world. This subchapter explores how to leverage ServiceNow's integration capabilities to connect your instance with various third-party applications, fostering a more unified and automated IT environment. By integrating ServiceNow with external systems, you can streamline workflows, eliminate data silos, and empower your IT teams to operate with greater efficiency.

The Integration Advantage:

Integrating ServiceNow with third-party applications offers a multitude of benefits:

- **Streamlined Workflows:** Automate tasks that involve data exchange between ServiceNow and other systems. This eliminates manual data entry and reduces the risk of errors associated with repetitive tasks.

- **Eliminated Data Silos:** Break down information barriers between ServiceNow and external applications. Integrations ensure consistent data flow, providing a holistic view of relevant information across your IT ecosystem.
- **Enhanced User Experience:** Empower users by allowing them to interact with data and processes within ServiceNow, regardless of whether the underlying data resides in another system.
- **Improved Decision-Making:** Gain a unified view of your IT service management data alongside data from other relevant applications. This empowers data-driven decision making and facilitates proactive IT management strategies.

Exploring Integration Options:

ServiceNow offers various methods for connecting with third-party applications:

- **Out-of-the-Box Integrations:** ServiceNow provides pre-built integrations for a vast array of popular third-party applications. These integrations are often straightforward to implement and require minimal configuration.
- **REST API Integration:** ServiceNow's REST API allows you to integrate with virtually any third-party application that exposes a RESTful API. This method offers greater flexibility but requires a deeper understanding of APIs and potentially custom scripting.
- **Use Cases and Community Resources:** The ServiceNow community provides valuable resources, including use cases and pre-built

integrations, to streamline the integration process for common third-party applications.

Establishing Secure and Reliable Integrations:

- **Security is Paramount:** Prioritize security throughout the integration process. Implement robust authentication protocols and data encryption measures to safeguard sensitive information exchanged between ServiceNow and external systems.
- **Clearly Define Data Ownership and Governance:** Establish clear guidelines regarding data ownership, access controls, and governance practices when integrating with third-party applications.
- **Monitor and Maintain Integrations:** Regularly monitor the performance of your integrations and proactively address any errors or disruptions. Schedule periodic reviews to ensure integrations remain aligned with your evolving business needs.

By understanding the integration landscape, selecting the appropriate method, and prioritizing security, you'll establish successful connections between ServiceNow and your third-party applications. These integrations will transform your ServiceNow instance into a central hub, fostering a more automated and efficient IT environment.

7.2: Building Custom Integrations: Tailoring ServiceNow to Your Specific Needs

While out-of-the-box integrations and pre-built connectors address many common use cases, there may be scenarios where you require a more specialized approach. This subchapter dives into building custom integrations within ServiceNow, empowering you to tailor your instance to perfectly align with your unique business needs and IT ecosystem.

Understanding Custom Integrations:

Custom integrations involve building bespoke connections between ServiceNow and external applications that are not supported by pre-built options. These integrations often require scripting and a deeper understanding of ServiceNow's APIs and functionalities, as well as the APIs of the third-party application you intend to connect with.

Scenarios for Custom Integrations:

- **Legacy Applications:** Perhaps you have legacy applications within your IT environment that lack pre-built integrations with ServiceNow. Custom integrations can bridge the gap and ensure these legacy systems can exchange data seamlessly with ServiceNow.
- **Unique Data Exchange Requirements:** If your integration needs involve exchanging complex data structures or require specific data transformations, a custom integration may

be necessary to tailor the connection to your specific requirements.
- **Highly Specialized Workflows:** For highly specialized workflows that necessitate intricate interactions between ServiceNow and external systems, custom integrations offer the flexibility to orchestrate complex data exchange and automated actions.

Building Custom Integrations with ServiceNow:

- **Technical Skills Required:** Building custom integrations typically requires proficiency in scripting languages supported by ServiceNow, such as JavaScript or Python. Additionally, a solid understanding of ServiceNow's APIs and the APIs of the target third-party application is essential.
- **REST API and Scripting:** ServiceNow's REST API provides the foundation for building custom integrations. You'll leverage scripting languages to interact with the ServiceNow API and the API of the external application to exchange data and orchestrate workflows.
- **Testing and Documentation:** Thorough testing in a non-production environment is crucial to ensure the custom integration functions as intended and doesn't introduce errors into your ServiceNow instance. Detailed documentation of the integration logic and data mapping processes is essential for ongoing maintenance and future reference.

Best Practices for Custom Integration Development:

- **Clearly Define Requirements:** Clearly articulate the purpose and desired functionality of the custom integration before commencing development. This ensures the integration aligns with your specific business needs.
- **Prioritize Security:** Implement robust security measures within your custom integration code. This includes proper authentication, authorization, and data encryption practices to safeguard sensitive information.
- **Leverage Community Resources:** The ServiceNow community offers a wealth of resources, including code samples and best practices guides, to assist you in building custom integrations.
- **Plan for Maintainability:** Write clean, well-documented code that adheres to ServiceNow's best practices. This ensures the long-term maintainability of your custom integration and simplifies future modifications.

By following these guidelines and possessing the necessary technical skills, you can establish secure and reliable custom integrations that extend the capabilities of your ServiceNow instance. Custom integrations empower you to connect ServiceNow with virtually any external system, fostering a fully integrated IT ecosystem that perfectly aligns with your unique business requirements.

Chapter 8: The ServiceNow Community: A World of Knowledge and Support Awaits

Your ServiceNow journey doesn't end with the implementation of the platform. An active and vibrant community surrounds ServiceNow, offering a wealth of resources, expertise, and opportunities for continuous learning and collaboration. This chapter delves into the power of the ServiceNow community, highlighting the various resources and channels available to help you unlock the full potential of your ServiceNow investment.

Throughout this chapter, you'll discover:

- **The Value of Community:** Explore the many benefits of engaging with the ServiceNow community, including access to knowledge, best practices, and peer-to-peer support.
- **Exploring Community Resources:** Uncover the diverse resources available within the ServiceNow community, including documentation, forums, user groups, and knowledge base articles.
- **Actively Participating in the Community:** Learn how to contribute to the ServiceNow community by sharing your knowledge, asking questions, and collaborating with fellow users and experts.

By actively participating in the ServiceNow community, you'll gain invaluable insights, stay informed about the latest platform developments, and connect with a network of passionate professionals who share your ServiceNow experience. This collaborative environment empowers you to continuously learn, troubleshoot challenges, and optimize your ServiceNow deployment to achieve your IT service management goals.

8.1: ServiceNow Documentation and Resources: A Treasure Trove of Knowledge

The ServiceNow community boasts a vast repository of official documentation and user-generated resources, serving as an invaluable starting point for anyone seeking to learn, troubleshoot, or optimize their ServiceNow experience. This subchapter equips you with the knowledge to navigate this rich ecosystem of information and leverage it to maximize the value you derive from your ServiceNow investment.

Official ServiceNow Documentation:

ServiceNow provides comprehensive official documentation that serves as the primary source of truth for platform functionalities, best practices, and configuration guides. Here are key resources to keep on your radar:

- **Product Documentation:** (https://docs.servicenow.com/) - This official website houses detailed documentation for all ServiceNow products, features, and releases. Utilize the search function or browse by product categories to find relevant information.
- **Knowledge Base:** (https://support.servicenow.com/kb?id=public

kb) - The ServiceNow Knowledge Base offers a searchable repository of articles addressing common questions, troubleshooting steps, and known issues. This platform is a valuable resource for finding solutions to specific challenges you might encounter.

- **Developer Network:** (https://developer.servicenow.com/) - Geared towards developers and those interested in extending ServiceNow's functionality, the Developer Network provides comprehensive resources, including code samples, APIs references, and best practices for building custom integrations and applications on the ServiceNow platform.

Community-Driven Resources:

Beyond official documentation, the ServiceNow community thrives on user-generated content:

- **Community Wiki:** The ServiceNow community wiki is a collaborative platform where users can contribute knowledge base articles, best practices guides, and troubleshooting tips. Search the wiki or browse by topic to discover valuable insights shared by fellow ServiceNow users.
- **Blogs and Forums:** The ServiceNow community ecosystem extends to various blogs and forums maintained by ServiceNow experts and enthusiasts. These platforms offer diverse perspectives, real-world use cases, and discussions on various ServiceNow topics.

Optimizing Your Search Strategy:

- **Leverage Keywords:** Effectively utilize keywords when searching for information within the ServiceNow documentation and community resources. Focus on specific functionalities, error messages, or processes you're seeking information about.
- **Combine Official and Community Resources:** Don't limit yourself to official documentation alone. Community-driven resources often provide practical insights and alternative solutions that complement the official documentation.
- **Stay Updated:** The ServiceNow platform and community resources are constantly evolving. Subscribe to official documentation updates and regularly revisit community forums to stay informed about the latest information and best practices.

By harnessing the wealth of official documentation and the vibrant community-driven resources, you'll equip yourself with the knowledge and best practices to navigate your ServiceNow journey effectively. This vast ecosystem empowers you to learn, troubleshoot, and optimize your ServiceNow instance, ultimately maximizing the return on your investment.

8.2: Engaging with the ServiceNow Community Forums: A Wellspring of Knowledge and Support

The ServiceNow community forums serve as a vibrant online hub where users from all walks of life can connect, share knowledge, and collaborate. This subchapter explores the advantages of actively participating in the ServiceNow community forums, equipping you to leverage this valuable platform to troubleshoot challenges, learn from others, and contribute to the collective ServiceNow knowledge base.

The Power of the Forums:

The ServiceNow community forums offer a multitude of benefits for users of all experience levels:

- **Access to Expertise:** Connect with a global network of ServiceNow users, developers, and administrators. These individuals possess a wealth of knowledge and practical experience they are willing to share.
- **Troubleshooting Assistance:** Encountered a configuration hurdle or a perplexing error message? The forums provide a platform to seek help from the community. Describe your challenge and leverage the collective wisdom of experienced users to find solutions.
- **Learning from Others:** Actively browse forum discussions to discover best practices, alternative approaches to common tasks, and insights into how others are utilizing the ServiceNow platform.
- **Sharing Your Knowledge:** As you gain experience with ServiceNow, consider contributing your knowledge to the forums. Answer questions, share solutions you've discovered, and help others navigate their ServiceNow journey. Giving back to the community strengthens the overall knowledge base and fosters a collaborative spirit.

Navigating the ServiceNow Community Forums:

- **Finding the Right Forum:** The ServiceNow community forums encompass a wide range of topics. Utilize the forum search function or browse by category to find discussions relevant to your specific needs.
- **Crafting Effective Questions:** When seeking assistance, clearly articulate your challenge, including relevant details such as ServiceNow version, error messages, and troubleshooting steps you've already attempted. The more specific your question, the easier it is for others to provide targeted solutions.
- **Following Forum Etiquette:** Maintain a respectful and professional tone in your forum interactions. Acknowledge contributions from others and express gratitude for any assistance you receive.
- **Staying Up-to-Date:** Subscribe to relevant forum threads or utilize forum notification features to stay informed about new discussions and replies to your questions.

Beyond the Forums:

The ServiceNow community extends beyond the official forums:

- **User Groups:** Consider joining a local ServiceNow user group. These regional gatherings provide opportunities for face-to-face networking, knowledge sharing, and discussions with fellow ServiceNow professionals.

- **Social Media:** Follow ServiceNow and community leaders on social media platforms like LinkedIn or Twitter. This allows you to stay abreast of industry trends, ServiceNow updates, and community discussions happening outside the official forums.

By actively participating in the ServiceNow community forums and engaging with the broader ServiceNow ecosystem, you'll tap into a wellspring of knowledge and support. The collaborative spirit of the community empowers you to learn from others, troubleshoot challenges effectively, and contribute to the collective ServiceNow experience. This not only enhances your own ServiceNow expertise but also strengthens the entire community for the benefit of all users.

Part 4: Advanced Topics

Chapter 9: Security and Governance: Safeguarding Your IT Service Management Processes

ServiceNow empowers you to streamline IT service management processes, automate tasks, and improve overall efficiency. However, with this increased automation and centralized storage of sensitive data, security and governance become paramount. This chapter delves into security best practices and governance frameworks for ServiceNow. Here, you'll explore strategies to:

- **Secure Your ServiceNow Instance:** Implement robust security measures to safeguard your ServiceNow platform from unauthorized access, data breaches, and cyberattacks.
- **Establish Data Governance Practices:** Develop a data governance framework to ensure the accuracy, integrity, and confidentiality of data within your ServiceNow instance.
- **Comply with Regulations:** Align your ServiceNow practices with relevant industry regulations and compliance requirements.

By prioritizing security and governance, you can ensure your ServiceNow implementation fosters a trusted environment for IT service management, mitigating risks and protecting sensitive information. Throughout this chapter, we'll explore essential security controls, data governance best practices, and compliance considerations for ServiceNow. By following these guidelines and establishing a security-conscious culture within your IT organization, you can harness the full potential of ServiceNow with peace of mind.

9.1: Implementing User Access Controls: The Foundation of Security in ServiceNow

User access controls are the cornerstone of a secure ServiceNow environment. They dictate who can access the platform, what actions they can perform, and the data they can view. This subchapter explores various user access control mechanisms within ServiceNow, empowering you to establish a robust authorization framework that minimizes security risks.

Understanding User Access Controls:

User access controls define the level of access granted to individual users or groups within ServiceNow. Effective access controls ensure that users can only access the functionalities and data they require to perform their assigned tasks, preventing unauthorized access to sensitive information or critical system functions.

ServiceNow's Access Control Mechanisms:

ServiceNow offers a multi-layered approach to user access control:

- **Roles:** Roles represent predefined sets of permissions that grant users access to specific functionalities within ServiceNow. Assigning users appropriate roles is the primary method for controlling access.
- **Groups:** Groups allow you to categorize users with similar job functions or access requirements. Roles can be assigned to groups, effectively granting the same permissions to all members of the group.
- **Access Control Lists (ACLs):** ACLs provide granular control over access to specific tables or records within ServiceNow. You can define read, write, and delete permissions for individual users or groups on a record-by-record basis.
- **Data Access Rules:** Data Access Rules enable you to restrict access to specific data fields within a table. This allows you to control the level of detail users can view for certain data points.

Establishing a Secure User Access Control Strategy:

- **Principle of Least Privilege:** Grant users the minimum level of access necessary to perform their jobs effectively. Avoid granting excessive permissions that could be misused.
- **Regular User Reviews:** Periodically review user access and ensure roles and group memberships remain aligned with current job responsibilities. Revoke unnecessary access or adjust roles as needed.
- **Separation of Duties:** Implement separation of duties principles whenever possible. This

involves distributing tasks across multiple users, preventing any single individual from having complete control over sensitive activities.

- **User Activity Monitoring:** Monitor user activity within ServiceNow to identify suspicious access patterns or potential security breaches. This allows you to take timely action if any anomalies are detected.

By implementing these strategies and leveraging ServiceNow's user access control mechanisms effectively, you can establish a robust authorization framework that safeguards your ServiceNow instance from unauthorized access and minimizes security risks.

9.2: Data Security and Compliance: Protecting Sensitive Information in ServiceNow

ServiceNow often stores sensitive data, including personally identifiable information (PII), financial data, and intellectual property. This subchapter delves into data security best practices and compliance considerations for ServiceNow, empowering you to safeguard sensitive information and ensure your ServiceNow implementation adheres to relevant regulations.

Data Security Best Practices:

- **Data Encryption:** Encrypt sensitive data at rest and in transit. ServiceNow offers encryption capabilities to protect data stored within the platform and while being transmitted to and from authorized users.

- **Data Masking and Minimization:** Consider masking sensitive data fields that are not essential for users to perform their job functions. Additionally, only collect and store the minimum amount of data necessary to achieve your service management objectives.
- **Regular Data Backups:** Implement a robust data backup and recovery strategy. Regular backups ensure you can restore critical data in the event of a cyberattack, system failure, or accidental data deletion.
- **Activity Logging and Auditing:** Enable activity logging and auditing within ServiceNow to track user access and modifications to sensitive data. This audit log serves as a vital resource for security investigations and compliance audits.

Compliance Considerations:

The specific compliance requirements you need to address will depend on your industry and location. Here are some common regulations to consider:

- **General Data Protection Regulation (GDPR):** If your ServiceNow instance stores data pertaining to European Union (EU) residents, you must comply with GDPR, which mandates robust data protection measures and user privacy rights.
- **Health Insurance Portability and Accountability Act (HIPAA):** For organizations in the healthcare sector, HIPAA

dictates safeguards for protecting patients' protected health information (PHI). ServiceNow deployments storing or processing PHI must adhere to HIPAA compliance guidelines.

- **Payment Card Industry Data Security Standard (PCI DSS):** If your ServiceNow instance processes credit card information, you need to comply with PCI DSS, which establishes security controls for protecting cardholder data.

Maintaining Compliance:

- **Identify Applicable Regulations:** Carefully assess your industry and location to determine which data protection and compliance regulations apply to your ServiceNow usage.
- **Regular Risk Assessments:** Conduct periodic risk assessments to identify potential vulnerabilities within your ServiceNow environment. Address these risks by implementing appropriate security controls and mitigation strategies.
- **Stay Informed:** The regulatory landscape is constantly evolving. Stay informed about updates to relevant regulations and adapt your ServiceNow security practices accordingly.

By adhering to data security best practices and maintaining a compliance-conscious approach, you can ensure your ServiceNow instance safeguards sensitive information and meets the regulatory requirements applicable to your organization. This fosters trust with your users and stakeholders and mitigates the risks associated with data breaches and non-compliance.

Chapter 10: Unleashing the Power of Data: Reporting and Analytics with ServiceNow

Effective IT service management hinges on data-driven decision making. ServiceNow goes beyond simply automating tasks; it empowers you to capture valuable data throughout your IT service management processes. This chapter delves into the robust reporting and analytics capabilities within ServiceNow, equipping you to:

- **Transform Raw Data into Actionable Insights:** Leverage ServiceNow's reporting and analytics tools to transform raw data into meaningful insights that illuminate trends, identify areas for improvement, and inform strategic decision making.
- **Customize Reports and Dashboards:** Customize reports and dashboards to visualize key performance indicators (KPIs) relevant to your specific IT service management goals. This allows you to monitor critical metrics at a glance and track progress towards your objectives.
- **Gain Visibility Across Your IT Service Management Processes:** Utilize ServiceNow's reporting and analytics to gain comprehensive visibility into various aspects of your IT service management environment, including incident resolution times, service request fulfillment rates, and overall service desk performance.

- **Empower Stakeholders with Data-Driven Insights:** Share reports and dashboards with relevant stakeholders, fostering a data-driven culture within your organization and ensuring everyone is aligned on key performance indicators and service management objectives.

By harnessing the power of ServiceNow's reporting and analytics functionalities, you'll transform your data into a strategic asset. This chapter equips you with the knowledge and best practices to leverage ServiceNow's reporting and analytics tools effectively, ultimately driving data-driven decision making and optimizing your IT service management processes for greater efficiency and user satisfaction.

10.1: Generating Valuable Reports and Dashboards: Transforming ServiceNow Data into Actionable Insights

ServiceNow captures a wealth of data throughout your IT service management processes. This subchapter delves into ServiceNow's reporting and dashboard functionalities, empowering you to transform this raw data into actionable insights that inform decision making and optimize your IT service delivery.

Understanding Reporting and Analytics in ServiceNow:

ServiceNow offers a comprehensive suite of reporting and analytics tools, including:

- **Reports:** Reports provide detailed breakdowns of specific data sets within ServiceNow. You can generate pre-built reports or create custom reports tailored to your unique needs.
- **Dashboards:** Dashboards offer a visual representation of key performance indicators (KPIs) through charts, graphs, and other visual elements. Dashboards allow you to monitor critical metrics at a glance and identify trends over time.
- **Performance Analytics:** ServiceNow's Performance Analytics module provides pre-built dashboards and reports focused on specific IT service management processes, such as incident management, change management, and problem management.

Generating Valuable Reports:

- **Identify Reporting Needs:** Clearly define the purpose of your report and the specific insights you aim to glean from the data. What questions are you trying to answer? What KPIs are most relevant to your objectives?
- **Leverage Pre-Built Reports:** ServiceNow offers a library of pre-built reports covering various IT service management areas. Review these reports to see if they meet your needs, potentially saving you time and effort.
- **Customize Reports:** Don't be limited by pre-built reports. ServiceNow allows you to customize reports by filtering data, selecting specific fields, and defining sorting criteria. This ensures the report aligns precisely with your information requirements.

Creating Effective Dashboards:

- **Focus on Key Metrics:** Limit your dashboard to a focused set of KPIs that are most crucial for monitoring your IT service management performance. Avoid information overload that can hinder readability and understanding.
- **Visualize Trends:** Utilize charts and graphs effectively to visualize trends and patterns within your data. This allows you to identify areas for improvement and track progress over time.
- **Customize Layouts:** Customize the layout of your dashboards to prioritize the most critical information and ensure a visually appealing presentation. Users should be able to quickly grasp key insights at a glance.
- **Share Dashboards with Stakeholders:** Share your dashboards with relevant stakeholders within your organization, fostering a data-driven culture and promoting transparency regarding IT service management performance.

By following these guidelines and leveraging ServiceNow's reporting and analytics tools effectively, you'll transform raw data into actionable insights. These insights empower you to identify areas for improvement, optimize your IT service management processes, and make data-driven decisions that ultimately enhance service delivery and user satisfaction.

10.2: Using Data to Drive Continuous Improvement: Transforming Insights into Action with ServiceNow

Data is a powerful tool, but its true value lies in its ability to drive positive change. This subchapter explores how to leverage the insights gleaned from ServiceNow's reporting and analytics functionalities to foster continuous improvement within your IT service management practices. By transforming data into actionable steps, you can optimize your processes, enhance efficiency, and ultimately deliver a superior IT service experience.

From Insights to Action:

Here's how to translate data-driven insights from ServiceNow reports and dashboards into tangible actions for continuous improvement:

- **Identify Bottlenecks and Inefficiencies:** Analyze reports and dashboards to pinpoint areas where your IT service management processes experience delays, errors, or high volumes of rework. Focus on metrics that indicate inefficiencies, such as long resolution times for incidents or low first-call resolution rates.
- **Prioritize Improvement Initiatives:** Once you've identified bottlenecks, prioritize improvement initiatives based on their potential impact. Focus on areas that will yield the most significant improvements in efficiency, cost savings, or user satisfaction.

- **Develop Action Plans:** For each improvement initiative, develop a clear action plan outlining specific steps to address the identified issue. This plan should include timelines, resource allocation, and measurable goals for success.
- **Monitor Progress and Adapt:** Don't let your improvement initiatives become stagnant. Continuously monitor the effectiveness of your actions by tracking relevant metrics within ServiceNow reports and dashboards. Be prepared to adapt your approach based on the data you collect, ensuring your efforts remain aligned with achieving your desired outcomes.

Data-Driven Decision Making:

- **Focus on Outcomes, Not Outputs:** Don't get bogged down in tracking activity metrics alone. While important, focus on measuring outcomes that reflect the true impact of your IT service management processes. For example, prioritize metrics like user satisfaction with resolved incidents over simply tracking the number of incidents closed.
- **Align Data with Business Goals:** Ensure the data you analyze and the insights you extract are directly relevant to your overall IT service management objectives and business goals. Focus on metrics that demonstrate progress towards achieving your strategic priorities.
- **Foster a Culture of Data-Driven Decision Making:** Encourage data-driven decision making across your IT organization. Empower teams to leverage ServiceNow reports and dashboards to inform their actions and continuously improve their workflows.

By adopting a data-driven approach and utilizing ServiceNow's reporting and analytics tools effectively, you can transform insights into actionable steps. This continuous improvement cycle empowers you to optimize your IT service management processes, enhance efficiency, and ultimately deliver exceptional IT services that meet the evolving needs of your users and organization.

Chapter 11: The Future of ServiceNow: Charting a Course Through Emerging Trends and Innovations

ServiceNow has established itself as a cornerstone platform for modern IT service management (ITSM). However, the technology landscape is ever-evolving, and ServiceNow is constantly innovating to stay ahead of the curve. This chapter delves into the exciting frontiers of ServiceNow, exploring emerging trends and groundbreaking innovations that will shape the future of the platform and revolutionize the way organizations approach ITSM.

Here, we'll unpack:

- **The Convergence of ITSM with IT Operations Management (ITOM):** We'll explore how ServiceNow is fostering a unified approach to managing both IT services and the underlying infrastructure, creating a holistic view of IT health and performance.
- **The Rise of Artificial Intelligence (AI) and Machine Learning (ML):** We'll delve into how ServiceNow is integrating AI and ML capabilities to automate tasks, predict incidents, and personalize the user experience within the platform.
- **The Expanding Reach of the Now Platform:** We'll explore how ServiceNow is extending its reach beyond traditional ITSM functionalities,

encompassing new areas like employee workflows, customer service management (CSM), and security operations.

- **The Evolving Role of the ServiceNow Citizen Developer:** We'll examine how ServiceNow is empowering individuals with low-code/no-code development tools to create custom applications and automate workflows, democratizing IT innovation.
- **The Continued Focus on User Experience (UX):** We'll explore how ServiceNow is prioritizing user experience by creating intuitive interfaces, leveraging gamification elements, and fostering a more engaging platform experience.

11.1: ITSM and ITOM: A Unified Vision for IT Management

Traditionally, ITSM and ITOM have operated in separate silos. However, ServiceNow is pioneering a future where these functionalities converge, offering a unified platform for managing both IT services and the underlying infrastructure. This convergence presents several key advantages:

- **End-to-End Visibility:** By unifying ITSM and ITOM data, organizations gain a holistic view of their IT environment. This allows for faster identification of root causes when incidents arise and facilitates proactive problem resolution by correlating infrastructure events with service disruptions.
- **Improved Incident Management:** ITOM data feeds into ServiceNow's incident management

workflows, enabling automated incident routing, faster diagnosis, and quicker resolution times. Predictive analytics based on ITOM data can even anticipate potential issues before they impact service delivery.

- **Streamlined Change Management:** A unified ITSM and ITOM approach facilitates a more streamlined change management process. IT teams can assess the impact of proposed changes on the underlying infrastructure, minimizing the risk of unforeseen disruptions.

11.2: AI and ML: Redefining the ServiceNow Experience

Artificial intelligence and machine learning are rapidly transforming various industries, and ServiceNow is at the forefront of integrating these technologies into the ITSM landscape. Here are some ways AI and ML are shaping the future of ServiceNow:

- **Intelligent Automation:** Repetitive tasks like incident ticketing, service request fulfillment, and basic troubleshooting can be automated using AI-powered tools. This frees up IT staff to focus on more complex tasks and strategic initiatives.
- **Predictive Analytics:** Machine learning algorithms can analyze historical data to predict potential incidents, allowing for proactive maintenance and preventative measures. This minimizes downtime and ensures service continuity.
- **Automated Root Cause Analysis:** AI can analyze vast amounts of data from various

sources to pinpoint the root cause of incidents quickly and accurately. This reduces resolution times and improves the overall efficiency of incident management.

- **Personalized User Experience:** AI can personalize the ServiceNow experience for individual users. For example, AI-powered chatbots can provide self-service support or recommend relevant knowledge base articles based on user queries.

11.3: The Expanding Now Platform: Beyond Traditional ITSM

ServiceNow is no longer solely focused on ITSM. The Now Platform is expanding its reach to encompass other critical areas of enterprise management:

- **Employee Workflows:** ServiceNow is venturing into streamlining employee workflows beyond basic IT service requests. The platform can now manage tasks like onboarding, leave requests, and facility access, creating a more seamless employee experience.
- **Customer Service Management (CSM):** The core functionalities of ServiceNow can be applied to customer service management as well. Organizations can leverage ServiceNow to manage customer inquiries, track service requests, and provide a consistent customer support experience.
- **Security Operations:** Security information and event management (SIEM) capabilities are being integrated into ServiceNow, allowing organizations to consolidate security

operations and incident response workflows within a single platform.

11.4: The Rise of the ServiceNow Citizen Developer (Continued)

Traditionally, application development has been the domain of professional programmers. However, ServiceNow's low-code/no-code development tools are empowering a new breed of creators: citizen developers. Citizen developers are individuals within an organization with little to no coding experience who can leverage ServiceNow's intuitive tools to build custom applications and automate workflows. This democratization of IT innovation offers several benefits:

- **Faster Innovation:** Citizen developers can quickly prototype and deploy solutions to address specific business needs, eliminating the need to wait for overburdened IT development teams.
- **Improved Agility:** Organizations can adapt to changing requirements more readily with citizen developers able to build and modify applications as needed, fostering greater business agility.
- **Enhanced User Experience:** Citizen developers, often being closer to the business processes they aim to improve, can design applications that directly address user pain points, leading to a more intuitive and user-friendly experience.
- **Reduced Development Costs:** Citizen development empowers organizations to

create custom solutions without relying solely on professional developers, potentially reducing overall development costs.

11.5: Prioritizing User Experience: A ServiceNow Imperative

In today's user-centric world, a positive user experience (UX) is no longer a nicety; it's a necessity. ServiceNow recognizes this and is continuously refining the platform to provide an intuitive, engaging, and user-friendly experience. Here are some ways ServiceNow is prioritizing UX:

- **Modern User Interface:** The ServiceNow interface is designed with a clean and modern aesthetic, making it easy for users to navigate and find the information they need quickly.
- **Intuitive Workflows:** ServiceNow workflows are designed to be logical and easy to follow, minimizing the learning curve for new users.
- **Gamification Elements:** ServiceNow incorporates gamification elements like leaderboards and badges to motivate users and make completing tasks more engaging.
- **Personalization:** The platform can be personalized to individual user preferences and roles, ensuring each user has a tailored experience that aligns with their specific needs.
- **Seamless Mobile Experience:** ServiceNow offers a robust mobile application, allowing users to access the platform and complete tasks on the go, further enhancing user convenience.

Looking Ahead: The Future of ServiceNow

ServiceNow is poised to remain at the forefront of IT service management innovation. By staying abreast of emerging trends, embracing AI and ML, and empowering citizen developers, ServiceNow will continue to evolve into a comprehensive platform for managing all aspects of an organization's digital transformation journey. As technology continues to advance, ServiceNow's commitment to user experience ensures the platform remains intuitive, engaging, and accessible to users of all technical backgrounds. The future of ServiceNow is bright, promising to revolutionize the way organizations approach IT service management and unlock new levels of efficiency, agility, and user satisfaction.

Conclusion: The Power of ServiceNow: A Platform for Transformation and Success

Throughout this book, we've embarked on a comprehensive exploration of ServiceNow, the industry-leading platform for IT service management (ITSM). We've delved into its core functionalities, explored best practices for implementation, and unveiled the exciting potential of ServiceNow's future iterations.

As we approach the conclusion, let's recap the key takeaways that solidify ServiceNow's position as a transformative force in the IT landscape:

- **Streamlining IT Service Delivery:** ServiceNow empowers organizations to automate workflows, centralize service requests, and implement standardized processes, ultimately streamlining IT service delivery and enhancing user satisfaction.
- **Boosting Efficiency and Productivity:** By automating repetitive tasks and fostering a self-service approach, ServiceNow frees up IT staff to focus on strategic initiatives and complex problem solving, leading to increased efficiency and improved productivity within the IT organization.
- **Data-Driven Decision Making:** ServiceNow's robust reporting and analytics capabilities equip you with valuable insights into your IT service management processes. This data

empowers you to identify areas for improvement, optimize workflows, and make data-driven decisions that enhance service delivery.

- **A Foundation for Continuous Improvement:** ServiceNow is not a static platform; it's a springboard for continuous improvement. By leveraging ServiceNow's functionalities and embracing a data-driven approach, organizations can establish a culture of continuous improvement, ensuring their IT service management practices remain optimized and aligned with evolving business needs.

Beyond ITSM: The Expanding Horizons of ServiceNow

We've also explored how ServiceNow is transcending its ITSM roots, venturing into new territories:

- **Employee Workflows:** ServiceNow streamlines employee workflows beyond IT service requests, fostering a more seamless employee experience.
- **Customer Service Management:** The platform's core functionalities can be applied to manage customer inquiries and provide consistent customer support.
- **Security Operations:** ServiceNow integrates security information and event management (SIEM) capabilities, consolidating security operations within a single platform.

This expansion highlights ServiceNow's potential to serve as a comprehensive platform for managing various aspects of an organization's digital transformation journey.

The Future of ServiceNow: A Collaborative Ecosystem

The ServiceNow community plays a vital role in the platform's ongoing evolution. By actively participating in forums, user groups, and social media discussions, you can tap into a wealth of knowledge, share best practices, and contribute to the collective ServiceNow expertise. This collaborative spirit fosters innovation and ensures ServiceNow remains at the forefront of IT service management advancements.

In Closing: Harnessing the Power of ServiceNow

ServiceNow is more than just software; it's a strategic partner in achieving IT service management excellence. By understanding its core functionalities, implementing best practices, and embracing its potential for continuous improvement, you can leverage ServiceNow to drive efficiency, enhance user satisfaction, and empower your organization to thrive in the ever-evolving digital landscape. The future of IT service management is bright, and ServiceNow is poised to be the guiding light on this transformative journey.

Recap and Final Thoughts

This journey through ServiceNow has equipped you to harness the power of this industry-leading platform and transform your IT service management (ITSM) practices. Here's a quick recap of the valuable insights we've covered:

- **ServiceNow streamlines IT service delivery** by automating workflows, centralizing requests, and standardizing processes, leading to happier users and a more efficient IT team.
- **Boosting efficiency and productivity** is a core strength. By automating repetitive tasks and fostering self-service, IT staff can focus on strategic initiatives and complex problem-solving.
- **Data-driven decision making** is central to ServiceNow's philosophy. Robust reporting and analytics provide valuable insights to identify areas for improvement, optimize workflows, and make data-driven decisions for enhanced service delivery.
- **A foundation for continuous improvement** is established through ServiceNow. By leveraging its functionalities and embracing a data-driven approach, organizations can create a culture of continuous improvement, ensuring their ITSM practices remain optimized and aligned with evolving needs.

We also explored how ServiceNow is **expanding beyond ITSM**, venturing into:

- **Employee workflows:** Streamlining tasks like onboarding and leave requests for a more seamless employee experience.
- **Customer service management (CSM):** Applying ServiceNow's core functionalities to manage customer inquiries and provide consistent customer support.
- **Security operations:** Integrating security information and event management (SIEM) capabilities to consolidate security operations within a single platform.

This expansion positions ServiceNow as a comprehensive platform for managing various aspects of an organization's digital transformation.

Final Thoughts: A Collaborative Future

The ServiceNow community is a vibrant ecosystem that fuels the platform's ongoing evolution. Actively participating in forums, user groups, and social media discussions allows you to tap into a wealth of knowledge, share best practices, and contribute to the collective ServiceNow expertise. This collaborative spirit fosters innovation and ensures ServiceNow remains at the forefront of IT service management advancements.

As you move forward with your ServiceNow journey, remember this: ServiceNow is more than software; it's a strategic partner in achieving IT service management excellence. By effectively utilizing its functionalities, embracing best practices, and fostering a culture of continuous improvement, you can leverage ServiceNow to drive efficiency, enhance user satisfaction, and empower your organization to thrive in the ever-changing digital landscape. The future of ITSM is bright, and with ServiceNow as your guide, you're well-positioned to navigate this transformative journey successfully.

Resources for Continued Learning on ServiceNow: Deepen Your Expertise

Your exploration of ServiceNow doesn't end here! This list provides a comprehensive range of resources to keep you engaged and expand your ServiceNow knowledge base:

Official ServiceNow Resources:

- **ServiceNow Documentation:** (https://docs.servicenow.com/) - The official source for detailed documentation covering all ServiceNow products, features, and releases. Utilize the search function or browse by category to find relevant information.
- **Knowledge Base:** (https://support.servicenow.com/kb?id=public_kb) - A searchable repository of articles addressing common questions, troubleshooting steps, and known issues. This platform is invaluable for finding solutions to specific challenges you might encounter.
- **Developer Network:** (https://developer.servicenow.com/) - Geared towards developers and those interested in extending ServiceNow's functionality. The Developer Network offers comprehensive resources like code samples, API references, and best practices for building custom integrations and applications.

- **ServiceNow Community:**
  (https://www.servicenow.com/community/) -
  The official ServiceNow community forum.
  Connect with a global network of ServiceNow
  users, developers, and administrators. Engage
  in discussions, seek help, and share your
  knowledge to contribute to the collective
  ServiceNow experience.
- **ServiceNow Learning Portal:**
  (https://nowlearning.servicenow.com/lxp/en/pa
  ges/servicenow) - The official platform for
  ServiceNow training courses and certifications.
  Invest in your ServiceNow expertise by
  enrolling in role-based courses or pursuing
  industry-recognized certifications to validate
  your skills.

Additional Learning Resources:

- **Books and eBooks:** Numerous books and
  eBooks delve into various aspects of
  ServiceNow implementation, configuration, and
  best practices. Explore titles on specific
  ServiceNow modules or general ITSM
  principles using ServiceNow.
- **Blogs and Articles:** Stay informed about
  industry trends, ServiceNow updates, and best
  practices by following blogs and articles from
  ServiceNow experts and enthusiasts. Search
  for reputable sources and publications focused
  on the ServiceNow ecosystem.
- **YouTube Channels:** Several YouTube
  channels offer tutorials, demonstrations, and
  in-depth discussions on using ServiceNow
  effectively. These channels often cater to

different experience levels, so you can find content tailored to your needs.

- **Podcasts:** Expand your ServiceNow knowledge on the go by listening to podcasts featuring ServiceNow experts discussing various topics, success stories, and industry trends. Many podcasts are available on popular platforms like Spotify and Apple Podcasts.
- **ServiceNow User Groups:** Consider joining a local ServiceNow user group. These regional gatherings provide opportunities for face-to-face networking, knowledge sharing, and discussions with fellow ServiceNow professionals. The ServiceNow community website can help you locate user groups in your area.

Remember: The ServiceNow ecosystem thrives on collaboration and knowledge sharing. Actively participate in forums, user groups, and social media discussions. By continuously learning, engaging with the community, and staying updated on the latest trends, you'll solidify your ServiceNow expertise and become a valuable asset in your organization's digital transformation journey.

www.ingramcontent.com/pod-product-compliance
Lightning Source LLC
LaVergne TN
LVHW051743050326
832903LV00029B/2695